EXPLORING THE
SUBATOMIC WORLD

Understanding
PHOTONS

B. H. Fields
and Fred Bortz

Cavendish
Square

New York

To Eliana, who can light up the world with her smile

Published in 2016 by Cavendish Square Publishing, LLC
243 5th Avenue, Suite 136, New York, NY 10016

Library of Congress Cataloging-in-Publication Data

Fields, B. H.
Understanding photons / by B. H. Fields and Fred Bortz.
p. cm. — (Exploring the subatomic world)
Includes index.
ISBN 978-1-50260-544-3 (hardcover) ISBN 978-1-50260-545-0 (ebook)
1. Photons — Juvenile literature. I. Fields, B. H. II. Title.
QC793.5.P42 F48 2016
539.7'217—d23

Editorial Director: David McNamara
Editor: Andrew Coddington
Copy Editor: Cynthia Roby
Art Director: Jeffrey Talbot
Designer: Stephanie Flecha
Senior Production Manager: Jennifer Ryder-Talbot
Production Editor: Renni Johnson
Photo Research: J8 Media

The photographs in this book are used by permission and through the courtesy of: Pictafolio/E+/Getty Images, cover; asharkyu/Shutterstock.com, throughout; Wellcome Images (http://wellcomeimages.org), a website operated by Wellcome Trust, a global charitable foundation based in the United Kingdom/File:Sir Isaac Newton. Wellcome V0006785EL.jpg/Wikimedia Commons, 6; Thomas Forget, 7; Public Domain/File:Christiaan Huygens, by Caspar Netscher.jpg/Wikimedia Commons, 8; Thomas Forget, 11; Public Domain/File:James Clerk Maxwell profile.jpg/Wikimedia Commons, 12; Jonathan Nackstrand/AFP/Getty Images, 14; Hulton Archive/Getty Images, 17; Thomas Forget, 19; Public Domain File:Cavendish Experiment.png/Wikimedia Commons, 20; Thomas Forget, 22-23; Johan Hagemeyer, Bancroft Library, University of California Berkeley, courtesy AIP Emilio Segre Visual Archives, 25; Topical Press Agency/Getty Images, 26; Public Domain/File:Niels Bohr 1935.jpg /Wikimedia Commons, 31; Thomas Forget, 32; Wellcome Images (http://wellcomeimages.org), a website operated by Wellcome Trust, a global charitable foundation based in the United Kingdom/File:Louis Victor Pierre Raymond, Duc de Broglie. Photograph by H Wellcome V0028118.jpg/Wikimedia Commons, 33; W. F. Meggers Collection/AIP Emilio Segre Visual Archives, 34; Robertson. Smithsonian Institution/File:Erwin Schrödinger profile.jpg/Wikimedia Commons, 36; Thomas Forget, 38; Friedrich Hund/File:Heisenberg,Werner 1926.jpeg/Wikimedia Commons, 40; George Frey/Getty Images, 44-45; Forestpath/Shutterstock.com, 47; File:Ernest Rutherford 1905.jpg/Wikimedia Commons, 48; The Air Force Research Laboratory's Directed Energy Directorate/File:Lasertests.jpg/Wikimedia Commons, 50; Andrey Bayda/Shutterstock.com, 53.

Printed in the United States of America

Contents

Introduction

I f you love science, it is probably because you love questions. And you probably love questions because they can lead to discoveries. This book is about one of the most productive questions in the history of science: What is the nature of light?

As you will discover, that question led different scientists to different conclusions. Some, like the great seventeenth-century Dutch scientist Christiaan Huygens, concluded that light was pure energy carried by waves. Disputing Huygens from across the English Channel was England's Sir Isaac Newton, who had concluded that light was a stream of tiny particles. No one anticipated that it might be both. But, as puzzling as that seems, that is exactly what it is. This book explains how that can be. *Understanding Photons* is about bundles of pure energy, particles with no mass at all that always zip along at exactly the speed of light.

They weren't called photons at first. In 1900, when Max Planck proposed such bundles in a formula that explained the **spectrum** of glowing hot matter, he called them **quanta** (singular, quantum). He didn't think quanta were real, but they made his mathematics work.

Five years later, Albert Einstein, in explaining a phenomenon called the **photoelectric effect**, became convinced that Planck's quanta actually existed. Before Einstein's work, scientists had made clear-cut distinctions between waves and particles. The discovery of the photon blurred the difference. Along with the earlier discovery of the **electron** and the later discovery of the **nucleus**, it opened the door to a new understanding of **atoms** and "shed light" on the nature of matter itself.

Thanks to those discoveries, we now know that atoms are swarming with subatomic particles. They absorb photons, produce photons, and would not stay together without photons, yet they don't "contain" photons in the usual sense of that word.

This book will take you on a journey inside matter and energy. You will follow the questions that led to our understanding of photons. And along the way, you will discover the remarkable technology that our understanding has made possible.

1 WHAT IS LIGHT?

Our planet is full of life because it is full of light. Plants use the energy of sunlight to grow, and plants provide food for animals. Humans and many animals use their sense of sight to find their way in the world.

But what is light? That simple question has driven human curiosity throughout history. No question in science has led to more discoveries. It has led not only to understanding that important form of energy, but also knowledge about the nature of matter and the forces that govern the universe.

Light and Color

Among the first to pursue that question were two seventeenth-century scientists who are considered to be among the most important of their time, or of any time: Sir Isaac Newton (1642–1727) and Christiaan Huygens (1629–1695).

At Cambridge University in England in the mid-1660s, the young Newton made some important observations about color. Until that time, the prevailing scientific view was that white light was pure, and something had to be added to produce color. Though that theory fit with common sense, Newton discovered that it was wrong.

In a darkened room with a hole in the window shade that allowed a sunbeam to enter, Newton took a piece of glass in the shape of a triangular prism and put it in the beam's path. The light emerged from the prism in a different direction, and it spread out much more than it would have without the prism. More important, when the light struck the opposite wall, it was no longer white. Instead, Newton observed a band of colors from red to violet, like those of a rainbow.

Newton had expected the change of direction (called **refraction**), since many people had observed that phenomenon when light entered water or glass at an angle. But where did the colors come from? The glass was clear, and furthermore, when sunlight passed through a flat piece of glass, it remained white.

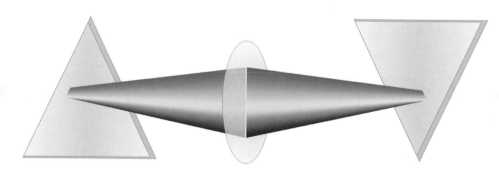

Newton's Prism Experiments. Through a series of experiments with glass prisms, Sir Isaac Newton discovered that sunlight is a mixture of all the colors that we can see.

Sir Isaac Newton (1642–1747). Generally regarded as the greatest scientist of his time, Newton studied many physical phenomena, including light and color. He hypothesized that light was a stream of tiny particles that he called corpuscles.

Newton investigated by putting a second prism, identical to the first but with its angle reversed, in the path of the refracted light. If the second prism caught the light of all the spread-out colors, then the colors came together and white light emerged. If the second prism captured only one color, then only that color and no other appeared on the other side.

Soon the significance of Newton's results became clear. White light is not pure, but rather a mixture of all colors from red to violet, which Newton called the spectrum. Today we call it the "visible" spectrum, because we know that the colors that we are able to see are not all the colors that nature has to offer. Beyond the ends of the visible spectrum, sunlight contains infrared and ultraviolet light.

Corpuscles or Waves?

But what is light made of? Because it travels in straight lines and casts sharp shadows, and because its beams **reflect** from mirrors like a ball bouncing off a hard floor, Newton decided that light must be made of tiny particles, which he called corpuscles.

Across the North Sea in the Netherlands, however, Huygens was more comfortable with the idea that light was a wave. In his mind, the refraction of light was a phenomenon similar to the way ocean waves, heading toward shore, change direction when they cross a submerged sandbar at an angle.

But how can waves cast sharp shadows? Huygens explained that if the wavelength—the distance from one crest to the next—is much smaller than the object the waves are passing, its shadow will be sharp. For instance, when ocean waves approach a very large ship from one side, there is a calm region on the opposite side. The larger the ship or the closer together the crests, the farther the calm region extends. In other words, the shadow is sharper since the waves don't fill it in as much.

Christiaan Huygens (1629–1695). Huygens's study of light led him to a different conclusion than that by Newton. He described light as a wave with its peaks and valleys so close together that it could cast sharp shadows.

Refraction of Particles

To understand how a stream of corpuscles or particles can refract, try this project. Take a wide piece of stiff cardboard, such as a poster board, and support one end of it on a few books so it becomes a ramp leading down to a hard floor.

Now take a marble or a similarly sized hard, small ball and roll it down the ramp, not straight along the center but at an angle. When the ball crosses from the ramp to the floor, notice that it changes direction.

A similar change in direction takes place when light passes from air to glass or water, an effect you may have discovered for yourself if you ever dove into a swimming pool to pick up an object at the bottom, only to discover that your target is not where you originally saw it.

So Huygens proposed that light is made of waves with wavelengths that were too small too detect, while Newton spoke of undetectable tiny corpuscles. Both theories could explain all known properties of light at that time, and both men were long dead before anyone came up with an experiment that might settle the wave-particle question for good. That experiment took place in 1801, and the person who performed it was English physicist Thomas Young (1773–1829). Young created a narrow sunbeam by passing sunlight through a pinhole. He then split the beam in two with a piece of thin cardboard placed edgewise. Instead of casting a sharp, thin shadow, as would be expected if the card had divided a stream of particles, the split beam produced a series of light and dark

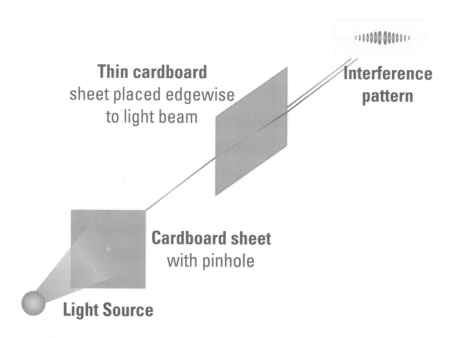

Thin cardboard
sheet placed edgewise
to light beam

Interference
pattern

Cardboard sheet
with pinhole

Light Source

Young's Experiment. In 1801, Thomas Young demonstrated the wave nature of light in a famous experiment. He split a narrow beam of light and allowed its two parts to come together. The result was not two spots as would be expected from a beam of particles, but rather a series of bands called an interference pattern, which would be expected from the meeting of two waves.

bands—an effect called **interference**. Interference occurs when waves meet. Where two peaks or two troughs meet, the result is a higher peak or deeper trough, which corresponds to brighter light. Where a peak meets a trough, they cancel each other, which results in darkness.

Young's experiment proved once and for all that light was a wave phenomenon—or so scientists thought at the time. But that discovery opened up new questions. A particle might travel through empty space, but surely a wave needs a "medium" to wiggle in, scientists thought. So they invented something called the "aether," and they concluded that it filled all space, even though it had never been detected. (If you're having trouble imagining what the aether might be like, don't worry. It turns out that light waves don't need anything to wiggle in—the aether doesn't exist. That explains why scientists could never detect it.)

Maxwell's Mathematics

James Clerk Maxwell (1831–1879). In four famous equations, Maxwell described electricity and magnetism as interrelated fields. His mathematics predicted electromagnetic waves that traveled through space at a speed that matched the measured speed of light.

One physicist who believed in the aether was James Clerk Maxwell (1831–1879). In 1856, he began his career as a professor at Marischal College in the city of Aberdeen in his native Scotland. Mathematical by nature, he began researching ways to describe electricity, magnetism, and the relationships between the two in mathematical terms.

Though his work in Aberdeen showed promise, his ideas did not come together fully until soon after he moved to King's College in London in 1860. By 1861, he had written down a set of four equations that are now among the most famous in science.

Not only did Maxwell's equations describe the relationships between electric and magnetic fields, they also paid an unexpected dividend. They suggested that a wave of **electromagnetism** could travel through space and even produced a formula for what the speed of such a wave would be. Astonishingly, that speed was almost exactly the same as the recently measured speed of light. Thanks to Maxwell's work, physicists now knew not only that light was a wave phenomenon as shown by Young's experiment—but they also believed they knew what kind of a wave it was. The aether, even though it had never been observed in any way, carried both electricity and magnetism. Or did it? Though Maxwell's writings described his view that **electromagnetic waves** traveled through the aether, his equations did not include anything that described the properties of that mysterious whatever-it-was.

Some physicists saw something in Maxwell's equations that Maxwell himself did not. Or perhaps it is better to say that they saw nothing where Maxwell assumed that something was needed. They argued that electric and magnetic fields could satisfy Maxwell's equations without the aether or anything else to support them—so why invent something that no one can detect? They were right, but it took more than forty years of scientific progress until the famous theory of relativity ended the discussion in 1905.

Even if physicists disagreed about whether the aether existed, they no longer argued about the nature of light. Sixty years earlier, as the nineteenth century began, Young had demonstrated the truth of Huygens's theory of light as a wave phenomenon. Now Maxwell's mathematics had shown that those waves were electromagnetic.

The case was apparently closed. Huygens had been right and Newton had been wrong. It was time to move ahead—to learn more about the way matter and electromagnetic waves interact. No one could have ever suspected that in the last year of that century, Newton's corpuscular theory of light would be reborn in a new form. And that discovery would lead to a new understanding not only of light but also of matter itself.

A Modern Aether

One of the most important recent discoveries in physics was the detection of the subatomic particle called the Higgs **boson**. In 1964, several scientists, including Peter Higgs, published papers in scientific journals that described how subatomic particles get their masses.

By then, scientists had discovered an entire "zoo" of subatomic particles. Many of these appeared to be quite similar to each other

but with different masses. They also had developed theories of the basic forces of nature based on exchanging a type of particle called a boson. For example, the electromagnetic force between two particles results from their exchanging photons with each other. Each basic force has its own basic field and its own type of boson.

Higgs and the others proposed that particles acquire their masses by exchanging bosons through a mass-giving field that fills all space, just like the proposed aether. Because Higgs was the first to mention the particle as well as the field, both came to be named after him.

Unlike the aether, which turned out to be unnecessary to understand electromagnetic waves, the Higgs field was needed to explain the different masses of otherwise similar particles. Detecting the Higgs boson required one of the most complex machines ever devised: the Large Hadron Collider (LHC).

On July 4, 2012, two teams of scientists using different detectors and experiments at the LHC announced that they had discovered a previously unknown particle that had all the properties expected for the Higgs boson. A little more than a year later, the Nobel Prize committee awarded the 2013 Prize for Physics to Higgs and another physicist.

Peter Higgs (*left*) accepting the 2013 Nobel Prize in Physics. Maxwell and other scientists incorrectly assumed that electromagnetic waves needed a medium called the aether, which filled all space, to carry them. Attempts to detect the aether failed because it does not exist. More than a century later, in 1964, Peter Higgs and other physicists proposed a different kind of "aether" to explain why subatomic particles have different masses. That came to be called the Higgs field and was accompanied by a subatomic particle called the Higgs boson. That particle was discovered in 2012, resulting in a Nobel Prize for Higgs and another physicist.

2 PLANCK'S
Surprise

I n the mid-nineteenth century, while Maxwell was using mathematics to discover that light was an electromagnetic wave, other scientists were exploring the atomic nature of matter. Though the existence of atoms was still a hypothesis, evidence was mounting that matter really was made up of tiny individual particles in constant motion. No other theory could better explain the way substances reacted chemically and the way gases behaved when heated or put under pressure.

Maxwell also contributed to atomic theory through his work in the mathematics behind the laws of thermodynamics, the branch of physics dealing with heat and temperature. He and others found that the best way to understand heat was by considering it the internal energy of matter due to the rapid motion of atoms.

Max Planck (1858–1947). In 1900, to explain the shape of the spectrum produced by hot bodies, Planck developed a theory that described light as being emitted in packets of energy called quanta rather than as a continuous stream. Though he considered it only a mathematical trick, it soon became apparent that quanta were real. Today we know them as photons.

A Puzzle in the Glow

One of the questions those scientists wondered about was the glow produced when an object is heated. How do hot objects transform their heat energy—the motion of their atoms—into light, that is, electromagnetic waves? Could they explain how, as its temperature rises, a heated body's glow becomes brighter and its color changes from deep red, to brighter red, to orange and yellow?

In 1895, the renowned Professor Max Planck (1858–1947) at the University of Berlin in Germany turned his theoretical skills to that question. Could he come up with a formula that

described the spectrum—the mixture of different colors of light—that radiates from hot bodies? Using a spectrometer, a device that spreads light into its component colors like a prism, scientists had observed the light that came from holes cut into the sides of very hot furnaces. Planck looked at the graphs of their experimental data, showing how the brightness varied for each color in the glow, and tried to find a formula that would match the curves he saw there in every detail.

To represent a color mathematically, Planck used its corresponding frequency (how fast the electromagnetic wave wiggles), increasing for visible light from the lowest frequency at the red end of the spectrum to the highest frequency at the violet end. He even used measurements of invisible light in the infrared (below red) and ultraviolet (above violet) regions.

Planck looked at graphs for different temperatures, and noted that all had one important common feature. Starting from infrared and going toward ultraviolet, they would rise to a peak and then fall toward zero. As temperatures rose, the light was more intense, and the peaks of the graphs were higher. The peak also shifted toward higher frequencies, corresponding to the changing color of the furnaces from deep red to bright red to orange to yellow. But no matter how hot the furnaces got, the measured intensity always dropped off sharply beyond the peak.

Planck thought about what kind of a model he could use to represent a hot, radiating body. It had to lead to a formula he could use to make a prediction about its spectrum. He settled on modeling the furnace as a collection of vibrating atoms, each producing electromagnetic waves according to Maxwell's formulas. He added those waves together to produce a spectrum and graphed it. His calculations yielded a remarkable match to actual data at the low-frequency end. But in the ultraviolet

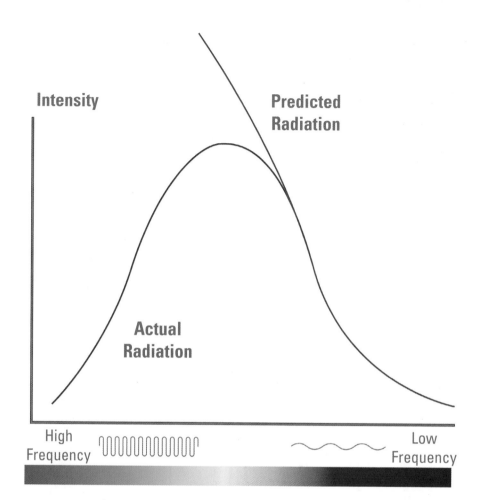

Planck's Quanta Save the Day. As this diagram shows, the predicted spectrum of a hot body without using quanta was very accurate for long wavelengths but failed miserably for shorter wavelengths at the violet end of the spectrum. Planck's addition of quanta produced a match at all wavelengths, eliminating what was called "the ultraviolet catastrophe."

region, instead of dropping off after reaching a peak, the formula predicted an ever-rising intensity of light.

Planck struggled to find a fix for the problem, and finally came up with what he considered a mathematical trick. What if energy was not like a fluid that could be measured out in any amount but instead came in discrete chunks (called quanta) like grains of sand? Each atom could vibrate with zero, one,

Nature's Fundamental Constants

When Planck was searching for a way to explain the shape of the spectrum of a hot body, he never suspected that he was on the trail of one of Nature's fundamental constants. Neither did he expect to transform the way physicists understood the nature of matter and energy. But we now know that matter and energy can be viewed as both wavelike and particle-like at the same time, and the mathematical relationship between the two views contains Planck's constant.

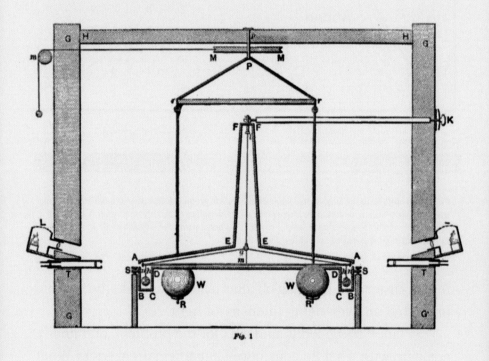

Fig. 1

Planck's constant turned out to be fundamental to understanding the nature of matter, energy, and the subatomic world. And it is not the only fundamental constant of nature. Other fundamental constants include a constant in the equation that describes the attractive force of gravity between two masses. That constant was first determined in a delicate laboratory experiment in 1798 by Henry Cavendish (1731–1810). Once people knew that value, they could use it to compute Earth's mass by the gravitational pull at its surface.

Likewise, two fundamental constants appear in Maxwell's equations, one describing the electrical nature and the other representing the magnetic nature of matter. When scientists realized that Maxwell's equations combined to describe electromagnetic waves, they found that the speed of those waves was a simple mathematical combination of those two constants. That speed turned out to be another of nature's fundamental values: the speed of light.

A Fundamental Discovery. When Planck proposed the light quantum, his formula included a quantity that was the ratio between the quantum's energy and the frequency of the light. We now call that Planck's Constant. He never imagined that the quantity was a fundamental constant of nature, just like the speed of light or the constant relating force to masses in Newton's law of gravity. Henry Cavendish determined the Gravitational Constant using the very delicate apparatus shown here to measure the force between the large balls and the small ones nearby.

two, or three quanta of energy, and so forth; but nothing was allowed in between the whole numbers, such as a third of a quantum, two and one-half quanta, or 17.76 quanta.

Planck realized that he needed small quanta at low frequencies, where his formulas agreed very well with measured spectra. Small quanta wouldn't change the results, he reasoned, since you can measure out almost any volume of very fine sand. But at high frequencies, large quanta—more like a pile of pebbles than grains of sand—would limit the possible vibrations and perhaps explain the falloff in light intensity at high frequencies.

Planck began with the simplest approach. He calculated the spectrum presuming a constant ratio between the quantum's energy and its frequency. Doubling the frequency would double the quantum's energy. Multiplying the frequency by three would triple the energy of the quantum, and so forth.

For each temperature, Planck adjusted the ratio between the energy and the frequency of the quantum to match the calculated peak intensity to the observed peak of the spectrum. He hoped by matching the highest point on each graph that the rest of the curve would also match fairly well, but the results astonished him. The peak intensity matched, as did the shape of the entire graph, all the way from infrared to ultraviolet. Even more surprising, the same ratio that made the curve fit for one temperature also worked for all the others.

Planck published the news of that amazing ratio, which today physicists call Planck's constant, in 1900. What began as a mathematical trick produced one of nature's fundamental values. But what did it mean? He and other physicists were determined to find out.

Naming the Photon

Although this book is about a bundle of electromagnetic energy we call the photon, scientists did not refer to it by that name for

more than two decades after it was discovered. Neither Max Planck, who invented it as a mathematical convenience in 1900, nor Albert Einstein, who first recognized it as an actual particle in 1905, used that term. They both called it a quantum or the light quantum (*Lichtquant* in German).

In the two decades that followed, scientists came to realize that the term quantum had much broader significance. By the 1920s, protons and electrons were well known as subatomic particles. The neutron, though not yet discovered, was also thought to

exist. But the word photon had never appeared until noted American physical chemist Gilbert N. Lewis (1875–1946) proposed it in a December 1926 letter to the editor of *Nature*, a leading scientific journal. The word quickly found favor in the scientific community.

Gilbert N. Lewis (1875–1946). Physicists did not use the term photon to describe the light quantum until Lewis proposed it in a letter to the editor of *Nature* in 1926.

Quanta and the Photoelectric Effect

The explanation came from an unexpected direction, a puzzling phenomenon known as the photoelectric effect. While Planck was pondering quanta, another German physicist named

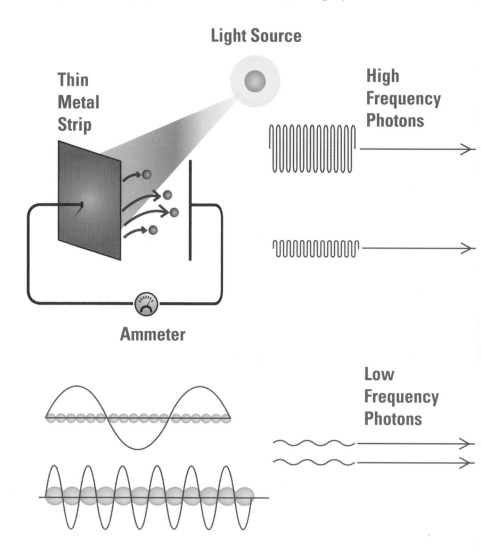

Philipp Lenard (1862–1947) had discovered that shining light on a metal could cause an electric current to flow—but only under the right conditions.

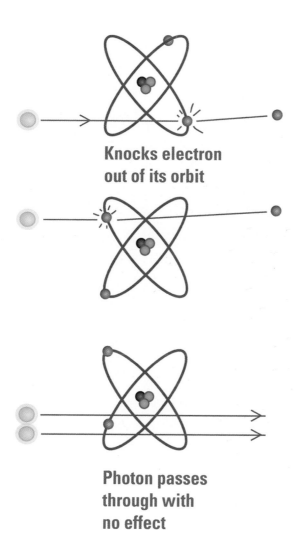

Knocks electron out of its orbit

Photon passes through with no effect

The Photoelectric Effect. At around the time Planck was proposing the quantum, Phillipp Lenard found another surprise called the photoelectric effect. Light shining on metal can, under certain circumstances, knock electrons out of a metal and create a current. The brightness of the light didn't matter, but its color did. Above a certain threshold frequency, no matter how dim the light, a current flowed. Below that threshold, even the brightest light produced no current. Albert Einstein recognized that the threshold corresponded to the frequency at which a single quantum had enough energy to free the electron.

Albert Einstein (1879–1955). Einstein, who is generally regarded as the leading physicist of the twentieth century for his pioneering work in relativity and quantum mechanics, won the 1921 Nobel Prize in Physics for his explanation of the photoelectric effect.

The current was a stream of electrons, themselves newly discovered in 1897 and the only subatomic particles known at the time of Lenard's research. Each metal had a particular "threshold" frequency for the light. At colors more toward the red end of the spectrum, that is, those having a frequency below the threshold, the metal did not release its electrons, no matter how intense the light. At higher frequencies, even the dimmest light would free some electrons. For most metals, that threshold was in the violet or ultraviolet range. But why should there be a threshold frequency at all?

In 1905, a little-known patent clerk in Switzerland named Albert Einstein (1879–1955) figured it out. Einstein knew that the minimum amount of energy needed to free an electron—the photoelectric threshold—varied from one metal to another. The threshold reminded him of a different phenomenon requiring a minimum amount of energy: Planck's quantum and the radiation of hot bodies. Einstein realized that if quanta were not merely mathematical conveniences but real packets of light energy, they could explain the photoelectric threshold. These energetic bundles, which later came to be called photons (see "Naming the Photon" on page 23), would not join together like a group of people to lift a heavy load. Rather, Einstein explained, a photon either has enough energy to knock out an electron all by itself, or the electron stays put.

Below the threshold frequency, no matter how many photons are in the beam—that is, no matter how intense the light—each photon simply lacks the energy needed to knock an electron free from the metal. Above that threshold, even a single photon has enough energy to free an electron, so even the dimmest light of that color can free electrons.

The Compton Effect

Einstein's explanation of the photoelectric effect quickly gained acceptance among physicists. Still, the photon's nature as a particle carrying both energy and momentum had not been observed in other ways. In a Nobel Prize–winning experiment, Arthur Holly Compton (1892–1962), observed what happened when X-rays struck a graphite target. (Graphite is a form of carbon.)

Compton noted that some X-ray photons had been "scattered." That is, they emerged at an angle away from the beam's original direction. He assumed that the scattering was due a collision with an electron. Knowing the mass of an electron and how much energy it took to remove an electron from graphite, and then using the laws of physics for collisions, he was able to compute how the energy of the outgoing photon ought to be related to the scattering angle.

His measurements agreed precisely with his calculation, showing that the photon's energy and momentum were related exactly as predicted by Einstein's formulas.

Arthur Holly Compton (1892–1962). Compton was the first physicist to measure the photon's particle properties directly. His observation of the way X-ray photons lost energy and momentum when they scattered off electrons is known as the Compton Effect.

By claiming that photons were real, however, Einstein opened up an even bigger question—or perhaps it is better to say that he reopened and transformed a question that scientists had considered closed for more than a century. Because of Young's experiment, everyone was certain that light was made up of smooth and steady waves, not a lumpy stream of particles.

Sixty years later, Maxwell's equations made the answer even more certain. Light waves were traveling electromagnetic energy. Planck's mathematical trick and Einstein's explanation of the photoelectric effect did not merely reopen the light vs. particle controversy, but they changed the form of the question from "either-or." Light was not *either* a wave *or* a stream of photons. Somehow, it was both at once.

In the decades that followed, that surprising experimental fact led to a new scientific understanding of the nature of matter and energy, and waves and particles.

3 LIGHT
and Matter

T hanks to Einstein and Planck, the old question "Is light made of waves or particles?" had to be changed. A new question replaced it: "How can light be both?" As scientists looked for a new way of envisioning light, they unexpectedly discovered that they had to do the same thing with matter as well.

Only a few years earlier, in 1897, British scientist J. J. Thomson (1856–1940) announced the discovery of the first subatomic particle, which we now call the electron. He and other scientists were puzzled by its tiny mass, which far less than the mass of the smallest atom: hydrogen. They also wondered what makes up the rest of atoms, and how the parts of atoms fit together.

By 1911, the best measurements had determined that the electron's mass was approximately $\frac{1}{1800}$ of that of a hydrogen atom. Meanwhile, the work of the New Zealand–born Manchester University professor Ernest Rutherford (1871–1937) had revealed the surprising fact that atom was mostly empty space, and most of its mass was concentrated in a compact, tiny nucleus.

Rutherford described the atom as a miniature solar system with the nucleus as the Sun and the electrons as planets orbiting around it, held in place by electrical forces rather than gravity. But Rutherford's model had one very serious problem. According to Maxwell's equations, the orbiting electrons would radiate electromagnetic waves. That would cause them to lose energy and spiral into the nucleus. Rutherford's planetary model was unstable.

Bohr's Model of the Atom

In 1913, Danish physicist Niels Henrik Bohr (1885–1962) found a way out of the instability problem, and it involved the photon. He was trying to understand the spectra produced when electricity passed through tubes filled with particular

Niels Bohr (1885–1962). Our modern understanding of energy levels in atoms is the result of Bohr's theory that explained the line spectrum of the hydrogen atom.

Emission Spectrum

Absorption Spectrum

Line Spectra of Hydrogen. When hydrogen gas is made to glow or allowed to absorb light, the result is a spectrum with a series of lines at different frequencies. Bohr's energy levels successfully predicted the patterns seen here. Glowing hydrogen emits light with those frequencies (*upper spectrum*). Cooler hydrogen, such as in the atmosphere of a star, absorbs those frequencies as the starlight passes through, producing a series of dark lines (*lower spectrum*).

gases. The light from those tubes was quite different from the continuous band of colors that Newton had seen when he passed sunlight through a glass prism.

Instead of a prism, scientists used devices called spectroscopes, which spread out the colors from the glowing tubes into a spectrum. Instead of a band of colors, the spectroscopes produced a series of sharp lines separated by darkness. Each line corresponded to a particular wavelength or color. Each gas glowed in its own pattern of particular wavelengths.

The hydrogen spectrum was particularly interesting because it contained several sets of colored lines in which the wavelengths obeyed a simple mathematical relationship. Since the hydrogen atom was uncomplicated—just one electron in orbit around a nucleus—Bohr hoped to develop a theory from the hydrogen spectrum that would uncover the physical phenomena underlying the mathematical patterns.

Bohr made some shrewd guesses about electron orbits. He proposed that nature allowed electrons in atoms to have only certain natural orbits in which they can move without radiating. It was as if the planets of the solar system could orbit only at certain specific distances from the sun and nowhere in between.

Using Maxwell's Equations and the laws of planetary motion, he was able to compute the ratio of the electron's energy to its frequency of rotation in those orbits. In the allowed orbits, that ratio was a whole number multiple of Planck's constant. No other orbits could exist. When an electron drops from one of those natural orbits to another with lower energy, the energy difference appears as a quantum. Bohr calculated the frequencies of light that would result from hydrogen's natural orbits, and the results matched sets of lines in the hydrogen spectrum.

Other physicists, most notably Arnold Sommerfeld (1868–1951) of Germany, extended Bohr's work beyond circular orbits to include elliptical ones, like those of the actual planets in the Solar System. With those insights, the planetary model of the atom was making more sense. But there was still a lot of additional work to do, and that would require scientists to revamp some of their most basic ideas, including completely eliminating the sharp distinction between particles and waves for matter as well as light.

Electrons As Waves

If light, long to be thought of as a wave phenomenon, could sometimes behave like a stream of particles, could particles like electrons sometimes behave like waves?

Patterns in the Hydrogen Spectrum

Like any other new idea in science, Bohr's prediction of **energy levels** in the hydrogen atom was accepted only when it fit with experiments and observations. In this case, Bohr was aware of the Rydberg formula, devised by Swiss physicist Johannes Rydberg (1854–1919) in 1888, that matched the observed wavelengths in the hydrogen spectrum.

Rydberg devised his formula to match a pattern noticed in 1885 by Johann Jakob Balmer (1825–1898). Balmer, a teacher in a school for girls in Basel, Switzerland, found a series of spectral lines whose wavelengths were multiples of 0.36456 micrometers. The multipliers for his series were fractions $9/5$, $16/12$, $25/21$, $36/32$, and so forth. The numerators of those fractions are a series of perfect squares beginning with 3^2 or 9, and the denominators are less than the numerators by 4. Thus 9/5 is $3^2/(3^2-4)$; 16/12 is $4^2/(4^2-4)$; and so forth. The first four lines in the series are in the visible spectrum. The rest are in the infrared range.

Rydberg suggested that there might be other series of spectral lines. He noted that 4 is equal to the square of 2, and suggested that Balmer's formula could be extended to other squares. By 1908, Rydberg's idea had borne fruit, with the observation of parts of two other series, one in the ultraviolet range (with 4 replaced by 1), and the other in the infrared (with 4 replaced by 9). Rydberg had no idea of why his formula worked so well, but experiments showed that it did.

The explanation came from Bohr's theory, which relied on Planck's constant. It produced energy levels that led to spectral lines with exactly Rydberg's values. The patterns found by trial and error now had a basis in physics.

Johannes Rydberg (1854–1919). Bohr's energy levels led to a set of wavelengths in the hydrogen spectrum that provided a physical basis for numerical patterns that Rydberg and Johann Jakob Balmer described in the 1880s.

Louis-Victor de Broglie (1892–1987). In his 1924 doctoral thesis, de Broglie proposed that particles like electrons could exhibit wavelike behavior, just as light waves could exhibit particle-like behavior.

In 1924, a French physics student named Louis-Victor de Broglie (1892–1987) explored that question in his doctoral dissertation. His answer was a clear yes. He devised a formula that used Planck's constant to relate an electron's wavelength to its speed, and discovered that the circumference of the allowed orbits in Bohr's theory was a whole number of electron wavelengths.

Now the distinction between particles and waves had blurred completely, and other physicists struggled to find new ways to understand the laws of electromagnetism and motion within the atom. Austrian professor Erwin Schrödinger

(1887–1961) developed an equation that, instead of describing a particle as if it is in one place, substituted a mathematical formula called a **"wave function,"** which described the probability of finding the particle in many different places. Schrödinger's approach launched a new field of physics called **quantum mechanics.**

Erwin Schrödinger (1887–1961). Schrödinger developed a mathematical blending of particle and wave properties into a quantity called the wave function. Just as Newton's Laws of motion describe how a particle moves under the influence of forces, Schrödinger's Equation shows how wave functions behave under the influence of fields.

To understand what the wave function represents, imagine an object bouncing back and forth on a tight spring so fast that all you can see is a blur. The blur is darkest near the ends of its motion where the object moves more slowly as it decelerates and changes direction, and it is least distinct in the middle where it is moving fastest. But where is the object, really? That's the wrong question to ask in quantum mechanics. All the equation can tell you is that the object is more likely to be found near an end than in the middle, because the object is the blur.

Schrödinger applied his equation to the hydrogen atom, and it produced a series of different wave functions—quantum states—that an electron might occupy. Each wave function was concentrated at a certain distance from the nucleus and was associated with a particular energy level. The distances and energy levels were exactly the ones that Bohr and Sommerfeld had calculated. But quantum mechanics had one significant advantage over the Bohr model. It didn't require changing the laws of electromagnetism for special orbits. Instead, it led people to a new view of electrons in atoms. Rather than being particles following particular orbits, they were fuzzy wave-function clouds occupying one of many "orbitals" within the atom.

The prediction of the hydrogen spectrum was the first of many theoretical triumphs for quantum mechanics, so physicists gradually accepted this new blurry view of subatomic particles. In Germany, Werner Heisenberg (1901–1976) realized that quantum mechanical ideas had great significance for understanding measurement. When scientists measure something, the precision of their instruments is always limited, and the number they get is never perfectly exact. They will say the measurement has "an uncertainty."

Heisenberg realized that minimizing the uncertainty in the measured position of an object depends on how well you

Werner Heisenberg (1901–1976). Heisenberg's approach to quantum mechanics took a different mathematical form from Schrödinger's but produced similar conclusions. His insight into the limitations of measurements, expressed as the Principle of Uncertainty, proved valuable in the development of quantum electrodynamics.

know its speed. Likewise, minimizing the uncertainty in the measured speed depends on how well you know where it is. He soon realized that the two minimum uncertainties were related—their product was Planck's constant divided by the mass of the object—and that quantum mechanics was nature's way to describe the limits on how well the two related quantities could be measured. Heisenberg found a similar result for the measurement of time intervals and energy.

Maxwell's Equations for the Quantum World

The Heisenberg **uncertainty principle** also turns out to be very important for understanding electromagnetic effects within atoms. Maxwell's equations had been developed to describe the electrical and magnetic interactions between particles whose location could be precisely measured. The equations described electric and magnetic fields that vary precisely in space and time according to certain mathematical rules. Inside the atom, quantum mechanical fuzziness made such precision impossible.

To understand photons and other subatomic particles, scientists needed to replace Maxwell's equations, which were the basis of an area of physics called **electrodynamics**, with a new mathematical formulation called **quantum electrodynamics**, or QED. The problem, physicists discovered, was that they needed a new mathematical vocabulary to express nature's language for QED. It was not until the late 1940s that American physicist Richard Feynman (1918–1988) of the California Institute of Technology came up with a language of symbols for QED, which are known today as Feynman diagrams.

Feynman's work also changed some basic notions about matter, energy, and nothingness, which physicists call "the vacuum." You have probably learned that energy can change forms but cannot be created or destroyed. Physicists call that the law of conservation of energy. But how can anyone be sure that energy hasn't appeared or disappeared without measuring it? The uncertainty principle forced physicists to say that if you measure energy for a very short time, the uncertainty in the measurement must be very large.

Feynman Diagrams and QED

The way physicists apply Feynman's ideas to electromagnetism is easy to illustrate but difficult to compute. This simple Feynman diagram shows two electrons, labeled A and B, moving along straight paths from bottom to top. At a certain time, electron A emits a virtual photon (the wiggly line), and that causes it to lose energy and change its direction of motion. A short time later, electron B absorbs that photon, gaining energy and also changing its direction. Between the **emission** and absorption events, the universe gained a bit of energy, but that energy disappeared too quickly to be detected. That virtual event causes the electrons to repel each other, just as particles with like charges ought to do.

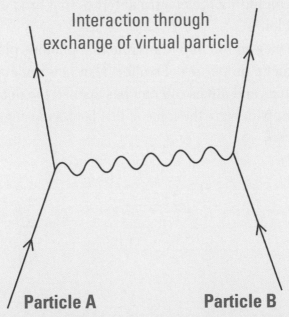

Interaction through exchange of virtual particle

Particle A   Particle B

Revisiting Maxwell's Equations. The exact form of Maxwell's Equations did not fit with the fuzziness of quantum wave functions. In the 1930s and 1940s, physicists struggled to develop a theory of quantum electrodynamics (QED) that would fit with the mathematics of both Maxwell and Schrödinger. They eventually devised a theory that was best understood by Feynman diagrams (named after the physicist who first drew them). This one shows the electromagnetic interaction of two particles through the exchange of a virtual photon.

Feynman described it this way: the vacuum is not perfect emptiness. Rather it is full of "virtual" photons and particles that flicker into and out of existence so quickly that any appearance or disappearance of energy is undetectable according to the uncertainty principle. The electromagnetic force is the result of the interactions between electrically charged particles and those virtual photons.

Feynman and other physicists worked out the ways to add up all possible exchanges of virtual photons between charged particles, producing a theory of QED that not only fit with Maxwell's equations for large bodies, but also worked for subatomic particles. More importantly, QED led to a new way of thinking about photons. They were not only particles of electromagnetic energy like light, but they were also the carriers of the electromagnetic interaction between subatomic particles—including the electrical forces that bind electrons to their nuclei.

QED showed the important role that photons play in the electromagnetic properties of matter. That new understanding of how photons and atoms interact has opened the door to new technologies, which are the topic of this book's closing chapter.

4 PHOTONS
and Modern Technology

U
nderstanding the quantum nature of matter and energy
has dramatically changed the world and society in
which we live. The discovery of the photon launched
a revolution not only in thought but also in technology. Much
of that technology is based on the flow of electrons, but the
photon has also played a very important role. The best-known
example of using photons in technology is the **laser** and the
many devices that depend on lasers.

But lasers are not the only area of technology where
photons play a major role. Other techniques and devices rely
on our understanding of the interactions between light and
matter—between photons and atoms. In this chapter, several
different photon-based technologies will be explored. But
first, we need a little more background.

Spectra and Spectroscopes

Hydrogen is not the only substance to have a distinctive line spectrum. Each atom or **molecule** has a unique set of energy levels, which means that each produces a line spectrum that is different from any other. Not only do they have emission line spectra that result from electrons dropping from a higher energy level to a lower one, emitting a photon in the process, they also have absorption spectra that occur when photons are absorbed and boost electrons from lower energy levels to higher ones. Physicists and chemists have devised a variety of spectroscopes (instruments that spread light into its spectrum) and spectrometers (instruments that measure spectra) to identify the atoms or molecules in a sample by the line spectra that they emit or absorb.

Those spectral lines occur not only in visible light, but also in electromagnetic waves with longer or shorter wavelengths, depending on the difference between energy levels. These include infrared light and microwaves at longer wavelengths and ultraviolet light and X-rays at shorter wavelengths.

In the long-wavelength spectra, the energy levels are often not determined by electron orbits but rather by other properties of matter. For example, molecules of a gas or liquid are free to spin around, but quantum mechanics tells us that the spinning rate can only take on certain values. Thus there are rotational energy levels, and the molecules emit or absorb photons whose energy corresponds to transitions between their different states of rotation. Likewise, because the bonds between atoms in a molecule can act like miniature springs, there are energy levels that correspond to different

False Color Image of Saturn. Spectroscopy has applications in many fields of science. This infrared image captures the planet Saturn while it is experiencing a strong south polar aurora. Its colors result from transforming each wavelength of infrared light into a corresponding visible wavelength. Saturn's infrared glow is the result of its temperature, so images such as this can reveal the temperatures and gaseous composition at different levels of its atmosphere.

rates of atomic vibration. Those occur in solids as well as liquids and gases.

Looking at the photons that result from transitions between different rotational or vibrational energy levels, chemists are often able to deduce important information about chemical bonding in different substances. That knowledge can guide them in their search for important new materials.

X-ray photons are also important tools for chemists and physicists. When an electron makes a transition between nearby energy levels, the photon produced or absorbed is usually in or near the range of visible light. But sometimes a high-energy event such as a sudden collision of a fast-moving particle with an atom causes an electron to make a transition

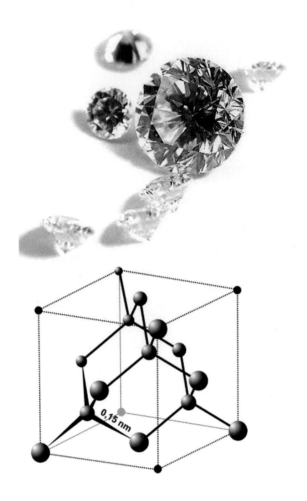

between two very widely separated energy levels, producing an X-ray photon that is characteristic of that particular atom. Scientists use X-ray emission spectroscopy to study the chemical composition of a sample material on a microscopic scale, and that is often important for understanding whether that sample is suitable for use in a high technology device or in explaining why a particular device failed.

Because X-rays have higher frequencies, or shorter wavelengths, than visible light, they are more penetrating and can reveal finer microscopic detail. Beams of X-rays

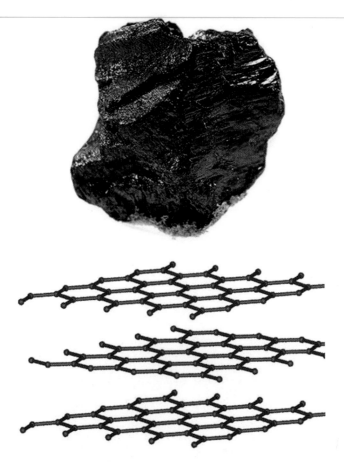

X-ray Crystallography. Because the wavelength of X-rays is comparable to the size of atoms, they can help scientists determine the spacing and arrangement of atoms in a crystal. Diamond and graphite are both pure carbon, but their atoms are arranged very differently, as shown here. Diamond (*left*) is hard because its bonds connect its atoms in a tight three-dimensional arrangement. In graphite, the carbon atoms arrange themselves in sheets resembling chicken wire. The sheets can slide easily past each other, which makes graphite both a good lubricant and the main ingredient in pencil lead.

are useful in crystallography, the study of the repetitive arrangement of atoms within a solid. X-rays reflect from crystals and produce patterns on photographic plates that enable scientists to determine the spacing between layers of atoms and the arrangement of those atoms within layers. That knowledge is important for making and understanding new materials.

Beyond X-Rays

X-ray photons carry a lot of energy, but one other region of the electromagnetic spectrum has even higher energy. The photons in that region are known as gamma rays. Gamma rays come from three very different natural sources.

The first gamma rays to be discovered came from radioactive materials, which Rutherford studied even before he discovered the atomic nucleus. Certain unstable chemical elements emit energy and transform into more stable forms. Rutherford recognized three distinct types of radioactivity, which he designated alpha, beta, and gamma rays from the first three letters of the Greek alphabet.

He determined that alpha and beta rays were high-energy particles. (Alpha rays are nuclei of helium atoms, and beta rays are electrons.) He found that gamma rays were similar to X-rays but with more energy. We now know that a gamma ray is a photon that is produced not by electrons but by the nucleus of the radioactive atom after it emits either an alpha or beta ray.

Just as electrons have quantum energy levels in atoms, a nucleus is comprised of protons and neutrons that occupy quantum energy levels within it. Emitting an alpha or beta particle may result in the nucleus having a proton or neutron in a higher or "excited" energy state. When the proton or neutron drops down to its normal state, the difference in energy is carried off by a gamma-ray photon.

Other gamma rays can come from outer space. When very high-energy cosmic ray particles strike Earth's upper atmosphere, they can lose energy suddenly and produce a gamma-ray photon. Another source of gamma rays are very high-energy cosmic explosions, such as supernovas. In 1991, the United States National Aeronautics and Space Administration (NASA) launched the Compton Gamma-Ray Observatory as part of its Great Observatory project. Its mission ended in 2000 when one of its gyroscopes failed. Other gamma-ray space telescopes have followed, and they have detected numerous gamma-ray bursts, the most powerful events in the known universe.

Gamma Ray Photons. Ernest Rutherford, shown here in his laboratory at McGill University in Montreal, was a pioneer in the field of radioactivity. Among his contributions was the realization that gamma rays, the most penetrating form of radioactivity, were similar to X-rays but carried more energy. In other words, a gamma ray is a very high-energy photon.

Lasers

The best-known technological achievement that depends on photons is the laser. Ordinary light of a particular color is made of many waves with the same spacing between their crests and troughs, but with the crests of one wave in no particular relationship to the crests of any other. Laser light is different from ordinary light and much more powerful because every wave is in perfect crest-to-crest alignment. Five unmatched waves produce a beam five times as intense as any one of them, but five perfectly matched waves produce a sharp and powerful beam twenty-five times more intense (five times five) that hardly spreads out at all.

How does that a laser produce such a beam? It is the result of a phenomenon called "stimulated emission of radiation" that occurs when a photon of a particular energy interacts with an atom. Suppose the atom would normally emit such a photon when one of its electrons drops from a higher energy level, called the "excited state," to its lowest possible energy level, called the "ground state." If a photon of that energy meets an atom with an electron in the ground state, that electron might absorb the photon's energy and jump up to the excited state. Once in the excited state, the electron would stay for a while before dropping back and emitting a photon just like the one it absorbed. That's called spontaneous emission.

Lasers for National Defense. Lasers range in size, power, and color, from tiny devices used to read DVDs or in handheld laser pointers to sources of intense beams. This optical engineer is evaluating the interaction of several lasers that will be used in a weapons system used to defend the United States against missile attacks.

But what happens when a photon of that energy meets an atom where the electron is already in the excited state? You might think that nothing unusual would take place, that the excited electron would drop back down and emit a photon at the same time as it would have ordinarily emitted a photon. That is not true. Instead of spontaneously emitting a photon at an unpredictable time, the electron reacts to the passing photon by dropping down and emitting a second photon in perfect alignment with the first, as if the two were members of a marching band in perfect step. Should one of those photons encounter another electron in the excited state, it stimulates that electron to drop down, and a third photon joins. In a laser, an energy source excites electrons in many atoms in the same material at the same time. Then as soon as one drops to its ground state and spontaneously emits a photon, a rapid chain reaction of stimulated emissions begins. In a flash (in both senses of the word), most of the atoms emit their photons in perfect alignment with each other.

That's light amplification by stimulated emission of radiation—the process that gives lasers their name. Laser light has many applications in technology because its beams can be very sharp and powerful and are yet are easy to modify and control.

Night Vision Goggles and New Light Sources

Other important technologies rely on the interactions between photons and atoms. For example, night vision goggles rely on materials that absorb photons from infrared light to raise already excited electrons to an even higher energy state,

Night Vision Goggles. This United States airman uses night-vision goggles to search for threats to his mission. The goggles detect infrared photons to create a visible image of the heat produced by enemy aircraft or missiles.

Photons and Modern Technology   **53**

from which they quickly drop down to a ground state and emit visible light.

The **light-emitting diode** (or LED) is another important technological device that is based on advanced materials with just the right set of energy levels. LEDs produce light in different colors and have many uses, including computer displays and household lighting. In order for those to be useful, they need LEDs that produce light in all three main regions of the spectrum: red, green, and blue.

Producing blue light from LEDs was a difficult technological challenge, but when the problem was solved, it was possible to produce white light with much less electrical energy than incandescent bulbs. Because nations around the world are concerned with global warming, caused in part by the burning of fossil fuels to produce electrical energy, the ability to make blue LEDs had great practical importance.

In part for that reason, the Nobel Prize committee awarded the 2014 prize for physics to three scientists whose work made blue LEDs possible. That accomplishment is just one example of many in which understanding photons is leading to a better future for all of us.

Glossary

atom The smallest bit of matter than can be identified as a certain chemical element.

boson A class of subatomic particles that includes the Higgs, the photon, and others that are the carriers of nature's fundamental fields.

electrodynamics A field of physics that describes the interactions and movement of particles due to electromagnetism.

electromagnetic wave A form of energy resulting from the interrelationship of changing electric and magnetic fields that flows through space at the speed of light.

electromagnetism A fundamental force of nature, or property of matter and energy, that includes electricity, magnetism, and electromagnetic waves, such as light.

electron A very light subatomic particle (the first to be discovered) that carries negative charge and is responsible for many important properties of matter.

emission Sending out something that has been produced, such as the emission of a photon from an atom when an electron drops from a higher to a lower energy level.

energy level One of many values of energy that quantum mechanics permits for a physical phenomenon, such as for the allowed states of an electron in an atom.

interference A phenomenon that occurs when two waves meet, resulting in some regions of higher intensity and some of lower intensity, in particular the light and dark bands produced when two light waves meet.

laser A device that produces a sharp, powerful beam of light by the process known as light amplification through stimulated emission of radiation.

light-emitting diode (LED) A device made of advanced materials that produces light of a particular color much more efficiently than incandescent light.

molecule The smallest bit of matter that can be identified as a certain chemical compound.

nucleus The very tiny, positively charged, central part of an atom that carries most of its mass.

photoelectric effect A phenomenon in which light can, under some circumstances, knock electrons out of atoms. Einstein's explanation of this effect led to scientific acceptance of the photon as a particle.

photon A particle of electromagnetic energy, such as light energy.

quantum (plural quanta) A subatomic particle with properties that have only certain allowed values related to Planck's constant. A photon is a quantum of light with energy equal to Planck's constant times its frequency.

quantum electrodynamics (QED) A formulation of electrodynamics that accounts for quantum mechanical phenomena, such as the dual wave-particle nature of matter and energy.

quantum mechanics A field of physics developed to describe the relationships between matter and energy that accounts for the dual wave-particle nature of both.

reflect The phenomenon that occurs when an electromagnetic wave strikes a substance and bounces off.

refraction The change of direction experienced by an electromagnetic wave as it passes from one material and into another.

spectrum (plural spectra) The mixture of colors contained within a beam of light, or the band produced when those colors are spread out by a prism or other device.

uncertainty principle Developed by Werner Heisenberg, a statement that nature provides fundamental limits on how well we can know two interrelated values, such as the position and speed of a particle.

wave function The quantum mechanical description that expresses the wavelike properties of a particle.

For Further Information

Books

Bortz, Fred. *Physics: Decade by Decade*. Twentieth-Century Science. New York: Facts On File, 2007.

Clark, John O. E. *The Basics of Light*. New York: Rosen Publishing, 2015.

Green, Dan, and Simon Basher. *Extreme Physics*. New York: Kingfisher, 2013.

Hagler, Gina. *Discovering Quantum Mechanics*. New York: Rosen, 2015.

Hamilton, Gina L. *Light*. New York: Weigl Publishers, 2009.

Koontz, Robin Michal. *Light in the Real World*. Minneapolis, MN: ABDO Publishing, 2013.

Whiting, Jim. *Light*. Mankato, MN: Creative Papaerbacks, 2014.

Wycoff, Edwin Brit. *The Man Who Invented the Laser:*
The Genius of Theodore H. Maiman. Berkeley Heights, NJ:
Enslow Elementary, 2014.

Websites

American Institute of Physics Center
for the History of Physics
www.aip.org/history-programs/physics-history

This site includes several valuable online exhibits from the
history of physics, including Rutherford's Nuclear World (www.
aip.org/history/exhibits/rutherford).

The Nobel Foundation Prizes for Physics
www.nobelprize.org/nobel_prizes/physics

Read about past Nobel Prize winners, including J. J. Thomson,
Ernest Rutherford, Louis de Broglie, Albert Einstein, George
Paget Thomson, Richard Feynman, and the inventors of the
blue LED. Each entry includes quick biographical facts
and brief summaries of their award-winning contributions to
physics.

The Science Museum (United Kingdom)
www.sciencemuseum.org.uk

This site includes the online exhibit "Atomic Firsts" (www.
sciencemuseum.org.uk/onlinestuff/stories/atomic_firsts.aspx),
which tells the story of J. J. Thomson, Ernest Rutherford, and
Thomson's son George Paget Thomson, who won the Nobel
Prize for his experiment that proved the existence of de
Broglie's predicted electron waves.

Museums and Institutes

American Institute of Physics
Center for the History of Physics
One Physics Ellipse
College Park, MD 20740
(301) 209-3165
www.aip.org/history-programs/physics-history

The Center for History of Physics houses a research library, a photo archive, and has created numerous online resources in all areas of physics, including Rutherford's Nuclear World (www.aip.org/history/exhibits/rutherford).

Ernest Rutherford Collection
Room 111 Ernest Rutherford Physics Building
McGill University
3600 rue University
Montréal, QC
Canada H3A 2T8
(514) 398-6490
www.mcgill.ca/historicalcollections/
departmental/ernest-rutherford

The Rutherford Museum contains the apparatus used by Nobel Prize winner Ernest Rutherford when he serves as professor of experimental physics at McGill from 1898–1907. The collection includes letters, documents, memorabilia, photographs of Rutherford and his colleagues, and other materials relating to Rutherford's work including the desk he used in his home.

IEEE Photonics Society
445 Hoes Lane
Piscataway, NJ 08855-1331
(212) 419-7900
www.photonicssociety.org

The IEEE, pronounced "Eye-triple-E," is the world's largest professional association dedicated to advancing technological innovation and excellence for the benefit of humanity. The Photonics Society is concerned with applying the science of materials, optical phenomena, and quantum electronic devices to invent and produce useful products.

Laser Institute of America
13501 Ingenuity Drive, Suite 128
Orlando, FL 32826
(800) 345-2737
www.lia.org

The Laser Institute of America (LIA) is the international society for laser applications and safety. Its mission is to foster lasers, laser applications, and laser safety worldwide.

Index

Page numbers in **boldface** are illustrations. Entries in **boldface** are glossary terms.

About the Authors

Science educator and consultant **B. H. Fields** has worked behind the scenes in the publishing industry since the mid-1980s, specializing in books and articles on the physical sciences and technology for middle grades.

Award-winning children's author **Fred Bortz** spent the first twenty-five years of his working career as a physicist, gaining experience in fields as varied as nuclear reactor design, automobile engine control systems, and science education. He earned his PhD at Carnegie Mellon University, where he also worked in several research groups from 1979 through 1994. He has been a full-time writer since 1996.